Napa

Vineyard in Napa

Wine, Food, and Fun: 3 Days in Napa Valley

By Jenna Francisco

Address:

Unanchor Press
P.O. Box 184
Durham, NC 27701
www.unanchor.com

Ordering Information:

Quantity sales. Special discounts are available on quantity purchases by corporations, associations, and others. For details, contact the publisher at the address above.

Orders by U.S. trade bookstores and wholesalers. Please contact Unanchor at hello@unanchor.com, or visit http://www.unanchor.com.

Printed in the United States of America

Unanchor is a global family for travellers to experience the world with the heart of a local.

UNANCHOR

Table of Contents

Introduction

=============

Are you planning your first visit to beautiful Napa Valley? Or have you been there before but would like ideas for how to make your next visit a perfect one?

This 3-day guide to this beautiful area of Northern California wine country provides everything you need, whether you're a first-time or return visitor. The detailed itineraries for each day give you all the essential information to plan your stay, with suggestions for where to stay, where to go, what to eat, how to get around, and of course, where to taste wine, as well as tips for how to taste wine and additional area resources.

Explore Napa Valley to its fullest, from the first-class restaurants and shopping opportunities in Downtown to the wine tastings across one of the most renowned and beautiful wine-producing regions in the world, this destination is a dream getaway!

What does your Napa Valley itinerary include?

- A 3-day step-by-step tour of Downtown & Napa Valley wineries.
- Detailed navigation information to guide you easily from place to place.
- Instructions for making winery reservations.
- Beautiful photographs of key sights.
- Dining, shopping, and sightseeing suggestions--meaning less time spent searching and more time spent doing!

What highlights will you see in Napa Valley?

- The Napa Wine Train
- Mud bath, mineral bath, & massage package at an extinct volcano site
- Wine Tastings
- St. Helena's Downtown
- Oxbow Public Market
- Downtown Napa

What is an Unanchor travel guide itinerary?

Each Unanchor travel guide is an itinerary curated by a local and includes a detailed planned timeline of sights to go see, maps & directions between each sight, as well as insider tips. The research work is literally already done for you. You just grab the guide and go start exploring now. No need to spend hours of time opening dozens of websites or getting buried under a pile of guidebooks and maps. It's like having a personal tour guide in your pocket but with the freedom to deviate from the plan and without the cost!

Are you right for this itinerary?

Both first-timers and those hoping to get a more in-depth Napa Valley experience will find this 3-day itinerary invaluable when it comes to planning out their trips. This travel guide includes 14 recommended bars and wineries, directions to every destination, and insider tips on how to make the most of your trip! It's like having a personal tour guide in your pocket!

Why You Should Buy This Napa Valley Guide?

- You will learn which restaurants and wineries to visit.
- You will get detailed instructions on how to get from place to place.
- You will have a great stress-free trip!

Guarantee

The itinerary will pay for itself the first time you follow my advice on dining and traveling destinations. My email address is included, so you are welcome to email me with any questions you have. And if you are unhappy with the itinerary for any reason, Unanchor provides a full refund. What are you waiting for? Get this itinerary and savor a fun and flavorful experience exploring Napa.

Day 1

============

10:00 am -- Arrival in Downtown Napa

- **Price:** $25.00 (for a single adult)
- **Duration:** 30 minutes
- **Address:** 600 Main Street, Napa, CA 94559

To begin our first day, we must first arrive in Downtown Napa, the city where our three days of Napa Valley exploring will be based. Park at your hotel or B&B and walk into downtown, or park for free on the street or in a nearby lot. The entire downtown of the city of Napa is walkable and has been redesigned to make the most convenient experience possible for visitors. With Downtown Napa as our base, we can walk to wine tasting, world-class restaurants, shopping, and accommodations. When we want to see the rest of the valley, we will need a car. There are drivers for hire in case you don't have a car here or prefer to not drive while visiting wine country.

Here is a map of our Day 1 Itinerary. Access the detailed online version here.

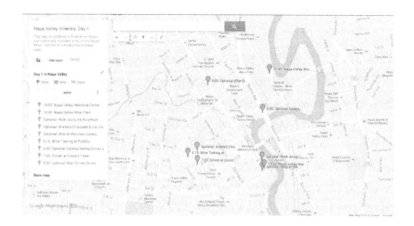

We will begin at the **Napa Valley Welcome Center**, where we will get two maps, one of Downtown Napa and one of Napa Valley wineries, plus our Downtown Napa Wine Tasting Card (cost = $25 for the card, which covers wine tasting at up to 12 wine tasting rooms in Downtown Napa). A free app is also available for download. Take advantage of the knowledge offered by the staff -- ask questions to help make your wine country experience the best fit for you.

You will need to decide which activity you will do next: the Wine Train or the Napa Art Walk + wine tasting.

10:30 am -- Drive to Napa Wine Train or Get Aquainted with Downtown Napa

- **Price:** FREE
- **Duration:** 30 minutes

1) If you are planning to take the Wine Train: Drive or walk to the Napa Wine Train, where plenty of free parking is available. See the Day 1 Map for directions, or go down Main St., take a right on 1st St., cross the river, and take a left on McKinstry. The 0.6-mile distance takes about 12 minutes to walk. When you arrive, get in line to purchase your ticket.

Alternatively, if you finish at the Napa Valley Welcome Center early: Drive or walk (about 8-10 minutes) to Oxbow Public Market, where we can also park for free. From the Welcome Center, go down Main St., turn right on 1st, cross the bridge, and it's on your left. This is one of the finest food markets in the region. We don't have much time before the Wine Train leaves, so for now we'll just get to know what's available here and maybe have a snack or coffee. We'll have a chance to come back and experience the market's specialties later. From here, we can easily walk over to the Wine Train.

2) If you plan to take the walking tour around Downtown Napa, you will begin at the Welcome Center on the Riverfront.

11:00 am -- Get a Sneak Peek of Napa Valley on the Wine Train or Get to Know Napa

- **Price:** $99.00 (for a single adult)
- **Duration:** 3 hours and 30 minutes
- **Address:** 1275 McKinstry St Napa, CA 94559 (or 1473 Yountville Cross Road Yountville, CA 94599 for Silverado Trail tastings)

(Note that prices begin at $99 per person.)

We are going to dig right into our three days in Napa Valley by taking the Napa Wine Train because it provides the perfect introduction to the region. The Napa Wine Train consists of wonderfully restored vintage train cars, and just riding in the beautiful and comfortable atmosphere makes this trip special. The food is another highlight -- in the spirit of Napa Valley's proud food scene, the train's chef uses seasonal produce, humanely-raised meats, and line-caught fish. Lunch onboard the train usually consists of a three-course meal with wine and coffee.

The train's route follows the tracks that were laid here in the 1860s to bring people to the famous hot springs of Napa Valley's northernmost town, Calistoga. The wine train begins in the outskirts of Napa but quickly becomes more and more beautiful as it goes farther north in the valley. The 1952 Vista Dome car, one of only ten glass dome train cars built, is my recommendation because its dome allows for panoramic views. If relaxing on the wine train is not enough activity for you, you can pre-book a winery tour. In this case, you will debark the train for the tour and re-board to return to Downtown Napa. Note that some tours mean a later return.

Alternative: If you'd prefer to explore Napa on foot, plan a leisurely walking tour through downtown. Use the following map as a guide and take your time, stopping in shops along the way. After the walk, continue to the Oxbow Public Market and grab lunch (644 1st St., on the other side of the bridge), if you haven't stopped for lunch yet.

First, start at the **Welcome Center** and go around to the Riverfront. Begin the **Napa Art Walk**, which takes you on an outdoor tour of fun sculptures made by Northern California artists. The works change every year, so if you come back, you will likely see different works next time. Continue along the Riverfront and down Main Street as indicated on the map.

As you walk along the Riverwalk, stop in **Liken** gallery to see the artist's work, fantastic interior design, and unusual flower arrangements. Peek into **Morimoto** next door for a glimpse of the high life in Napa.

Stop at **Molinari Caffe** at 815 Main St., just across from the Veterans Memorial Park, for a nutella latte.

Stop for wine tasting along the way. Use your Downtown Napa Wine Tasting Card.

Stop in **Anette's Chocolates** at 1321 1st Street for a decadent treat. This old-fashioned chocolate shop uses traditional and new recipes to create beautiful, high-quality chocolates and brittles. All sweets are made in this shop, and the aroma of fresh chocolates greets you as you walk in. Ice cream with chocolate cabernet sauce is another delicious choice. The fine products sold here, such as the dark chocolate assortment box, make great gifts to take home to friends and family.

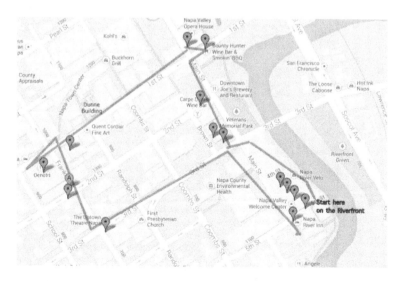

2:30 pm -- Drive or walk to accommodation

- **Price:** FREE
- **Duration:** 30 minutes

Now that we have arrived back in Downtown Napa, it's time to check in at our hotel or B&B. If you left your car at the train station, drive to the accommodation; if you parked at the accommodation, walk back there.

3:00 pm -- Check in and free time

- **Price:** FREE
- **Duration:** 2 hours

After checking in at our accommodation, let's take some time to relax before our evening plans begin! Let's take a look at the offerings on the Downtown Napa Wine Tasting Card, check opening hours, and decide where we might like to stop this evening.

Note: You may need reservations for dinner depending on how busy the season is. Phone numbers are listed next to the dinner recommendations for tonight, and now is a good time to call if you haven't made the reservation yet.

5:00 pm -- Walk to Wine Tasting Rooms

- **Price:** FREE
- **Duration:** 15 minutes

The great thing about staying in Downtown Napa is that we can walk to everything we need. Now let's put that wine tasting card to use. There are some great places on the other side of the river, near Oxbow Public Market and the Wine Train, but we'll be back on that side of the river on Day 3. For now, let's stick to the side of the river where most of Downtown Napa is located and stop at **pureCru** first (1463 1st. St).

5:15 pm -- Wine Tasting in Downtown Napa

- **Price:** $20.00 (for a single adult)
- **Duration:** 1 hour and 30 minutes
- **Address:** 1463 First Street, Napa, California

With our Downtown Napa Wine Tasting card in hand, we'll experience unique Napa Valley wines at the elegant Downtown Napa tasting rooms. Remember that the first tasting costs 10 cents. From here, we can make our way to **Square One Tasting Bar** (1331 1st St.). Map and addresses are provided with your card.

For a different drinking experience, save time to have a cocktail at **Morimoto Napa** (610 Main Street). This elegant and modern restaurant is run by Iron Chef Morimoto, and its innovative and beautiful food have become well known. Have a cocktail at the bar before continuing the evening for dinner -- they are expensive at about $15 each, but the flavors and atmosphere are worth the price. Alternatively, walk the pretty Napa Riverfront, which passes Morimoto Napa.

6:45 pm -- Walk to dinner in Downtown Napa

- **Price:** FREE
- **Duration:** 15 minutes

Walk to your restaurant of choice: Morimoto Napa (610 Main Street), Grace's Table (1400 Second Street), or ZuZu (829 Main Street).

7:00 pm -- Dinner in Downtown Napa

- **Price:** $50.00 (for a single adult)
- **Duration:** 2 hours
- **Address:** See choices below.

Because we're staying in Downtown Napa, we have many dining options. Let's choose one of these three recommended restaurants:

Morimoto Napa: the most expensive of the three restaurants, with the best sushi and possibly most innovative food you've had. Appetizers are $10-20, entrees $30-80, sushi and sashimi rolls less than $10. Open daily at 5:00 p.m.. 610 Main Street, 707-252-1600.

Grace's Table: my favorite restaurant in Napa. This "global kitchen" uses flavors inspired by traditional dishes from around the world as well as super-fresh and local ingredients, some of which come right from the chef's garden. First courses are $10-20, entrees $15-28. Open daily from breakfast to dinner. 1400 Second Street, 707-226-6200

ZuZu: a lively atmosphere and great Spanish-style tapas. Only small plates are served, from $4-15. Open daily at 4:30 p.m.. 829 Main Street, 707-224-8555

9:00 pm -- Walk back (or hit the town)

- **Price:** FREE
- **Duration:** 1 hour
- **Address:** Downtown Napa

Let's walk back to our accommodation, unless you still have more exploring to do. In that case, try **1313 Main** (1313 Main St.), **Silo's** (530 Main St.), or **Carpe Diem** (1001 2nd St.).

We've had a busy day, and there is much more to come tomorrow. It's time to get some rest and drink some water to counter all the wine we tried today.

Day 2

=============

8:30 am -- Breakfast

- **Price:** FREE
- **Duration:** 1 hour
- **Address:** See choices below.

Have breakfast at your hotel or B&B, or if you'd prefer, walk or drive to **Alexis Baking Company (ABC)** or **Grace's Table** for an excellent breakfast. ABC offers homestyle breakfasts ranging from $7 to $17; the stuffed pancakes with fruit topping are excellent. Grace's Table serves a fantastic breakfast including homemade pastries and flavorful egg dishes with prices ranging from $2 for a pastry to $12 for full plates.

Addresses:

- **ABC:** 1517 3rd St., Napa, (707) 258-1827
- **Grace's Table:** 1400 2nd St., Napa, (707) 226-6200

We will be on the road just after 9:30am.

Note: *Grace's Table opens at 8:30am on weekdays but at 9:00am on weekends.*

9:30 am -- Drive to St. Helena

- **Price:** FREE
- **Duration:** 30 minutes

We will take Highway 29 about 18 miles north to the town of St. Helena. The highway turns into Main Street as you enter the town. We will park on or close to Main Street.

10:00 am -- Small Town Napa Valley in St. Helena's Downtown

- **Price:** FREE
- **Duration:** 1 hour
- **Address:** Main Street, St. Helena, CA 94574

Let's get to St. Helena around 10:00am so that we'll be able to find parking. This small downtown can get packed with visitors by noon.

St. Helena is a small, pristine town in the center of Napa Valley. Its historic downtown is just a few blocks long and is loaded with beautiful shops and boutiques selling unique items. Even if you don't want to buy anything, we can have some fun looking around. A few favorite stops are **Napa Valley Vintage Home**, **La Boheme Resale Boutique**, and **Acres Home and Garden**. All of these are right on Main Street, so you can't miss them. The **St. Helena Visitors Center** is also located on Main St., where you can get a map or ask for specific recommendations based on what you would like to browse for in town.

If coffee is calling, **Napa Valley Coffee Roasting Co.** is a popular cafe among locals. It's is just one block off Main Street; go south/southwest on Adams St. and then right on Oak Ave., and it's right there at 1400 Oak.

Next up is olive oil and wine tasting, but if you'd prefer to skip that, you can meet us for lunch.

11:00 am -- Drive to Long Meadow Ranch

- **Price:** FREE
- **Duration:** 15 minutes

Long Meadow Ranch is less than 1 mile south of St. Helena, so we will back track down Highway 29 for just a couple of minutes and look for Long Meadow Ranch on the left (east) side of the road.

11:15 am -- Wine and Olive Oil Tasting at Long Meadow Ranch

- **Price:** $10.00 (for a single adult)
- **Duration:** 45 minutes
- **Address:** 738 Main Street, St. Helena, CA 94574

Long Meadow Ranch opens for tastings at 11:00m. Try the Essential flight of wine and olive oil tastings or, since you're in wine country, go for the Signature flight of reserve wines and olive oil.

Long Meadow Ranch produces food and wine from their large ranches in Napa Valley. They are committed to quality, sustainability, and organic farming methods. They host a farmers' market Friday-Sunday, offer food and wine experiences and family-friendly meals and tours. This is a good place to see another side of Napa Valley -- that it's not just about wine but also about top-quality, fresh food and produce that grows so well in this part of California.

12:00 pm -- Drive to Lunch

- **Price:** FREE
- **Duration:** 30 minutes

Drive on Highway 29 to **Gott's Roadside** just south of St. Helena, **All Seasons Bistro**, or **Calistoga Kitchen** in Calistoga (about 15 minutes north of St. Helena).

Option 1: Go just a minute or so on Highway 29 to **Gott's Roadside**. It's located at 933 Main Street just south of St. Helena.

Option 2: Head north on Highway 29 to Calistoga and eat lunch at **All Seasons Bistro**. Located at 1400 Lincoln St. in downtown Calistoga. *Closed Mondays.*

Option 3: Calistoga Kitchen is a small, modern restaurant located at 1107 Cedar St., Calistoga. *Only open on Friday and Saturday.*

12:30 pm -- Lunch in Calistoga

- **Price:** $30.00 (for a single adult)
- **Duration:** 1 hour and 30 minutes
- **Address:** 1400 Lincoln Ave., Calistoga, CA 94574

Try one of the following options depending on your preference, the weather, and the day.

Option 1: **Gott's Roadside** serves sophisticated diner food. The fish tacos, classic tuna melt, cheeseburger, and sweet potato fries are great choices. Burgers start at $7 and salads start at $10. The line here is sometimes long, especially on weekends. However, at Gott's, there is outdoor seating only, so keep this in mind if the weather is bad today (which is unlikely in Napa Valley). Gott's is open 7 days a week.

Option 2: **All Seasons Bistro** is one of my favorite restaurants in the area. The restaurant serves seasonal food with most ingredients, even the vinegars, made in house. Salads start at $9 and entrees at $11. Open at 12:00pm Tuesday-Sunday. Closed Mondays.

Option 3: Only Friday and Saturday. **Calistoga Kitchen** is a small, modern restaurant with a nice outdoor patio and overall excellent food. Salads start at $9 and entrees at $10.

2:00 pm -- Drive to Roman Spa or Solage

- **Price:** FREE
- **Duration:** 30 minutes

Drive to Calistoga and park at Roman Spa at 1300 Washington St., Calistoga, or Solage at 755 Silverado Trail N, Calistoga.

2:30 pm -- Calistoga Spa Treatment at Roman Spa or Solage, or Wine Tastings

- **Price:** $70.00 (for a single adult)
- **Duration:** 1 hour and 30 minutes
- **Address:** 1300 Washington St., Calistoga, CA

(Note: Reservations are needed.)

Calistoga was once the site of a volcano, the remnants now only the areas volcanic soil, geyser, and hot springs under the town. Calistoga was first settled in the 1840s because of its hot springs, and it's still known for the town's relaxed vibe and the water's healing qualities.

Popular spa treatments include a mud bath, which uses the nutrient-rich volcanic ash mud to heal the body, mineral baths, and massage. The one-hour mineral bath is a relaxing experience, but the massage followed by mineral bath is an even nicer combination. For those wanting to try the mud bath, Roman Spa offers a mud bath, mineral bath, and massage package. Prices vary depending on the service and begin at $70 for the one-hour mineral bath. 1-800-914-8957

Baths at Roman Spa are very nice -- clean, comfortable, and relaxing, if a little outdated. If you would like something more upscale, you can't go wrong with Solage Calistoga, (707) 226-0800.

Optional activities in lieu of spa treatments:

Address: 3340 Highway 128, Calistoga, CA 94515
Cost: $30.00

If you choose not to experience the Calistoga spa experience, there is plenty for us to do in the area.

Walk Calistoga's small downtown, stopping in its small shops and wine tasting rooms. Don't miss the old train cars and train station that have been renovated into small shops off of Lincoln Street.

There is enough time for us to go to a couple of local wineries. **Bennett Lane Winery** is the northernmost winery in Napa Valley, just a few minutes north of Calistoga. Reservations are required, but the outstanding red wines they serve are worth the effort. Tastings with a tour start at $15 per person. Call 1-877-MAX-NAPA to make a reservation.

Nearby **Envy Wines,** just north of Calistoga, is a friendly winery with nice red wines to try. The "swoon-inducing" wines of Carter Cellars are also available to try. Tastings start at $10 per person.

Nearby **Chateau Montelana** is worth a stop for its beautiful outdoor gardens, which can be accessed without wine tasting. This might make a nice place to walk before driving back to Napa.

4:00 pm -- Drive back to accommodation and then to dinner

- **Price:** FREE
- **Duration:** 3 hours

Let's drive to our accommodation and relax before dinner.

Be sure you've made a reservation for dinner at **Oenotri** at 1425 1st St, 707-252-1022. If Oenotri is full or you don't feel like eating Italian food tonight, try **Tarla Mediterranean Grill** instead (1480 1st St., Napa, 707-255-5599).

7:00 pm -- Dinner at Oenotri

- **Price:** $100.00 (for a single adult)
- **Duration:** 2 hours
- **Address:** 1425 1st St, Napa, CA 94559

One of only 5 restaurants in Napa Valley to be included on the Michelin Bib Gourmand list, Oenotri serves Italian food with local ingredients, some from the restaurant's garden. While all the food is excellent, the pastas and desserts especially stand out. Pizzas start at $15, pastas at $17, and meat entrees at $28.

Day 3

=============

8:30 am -- Breakfast at Alexis Baking Company or Grace's Table

- **Price:** $20.00 (for a single adult)
- **Duration:** 1 hour
- **Address:** 1517 3rd St, Napa, CA 94559 or 1400 2nd St., Napa.

Walk or drive to **Alexis Baking Company** or **Grace's Table.** ABC offers homestyle breakfasts ranging from $7 to $17; the stuffed pancakes with fruit topping are excellent. Grace's Table serves a fantastic breakfast including homemade pastries, yogurt and flavorful egg dishes with prices ranging from $2 for a pastry to $12 for full plates. ABC opens at 7:00 a.m. every day. Grace's Table opens at 8:30 a.m. every day except Saturday and Sunday, when it opens at 9:00 a.m.

Addresses:

- **ABC:** 1517 3rd St., Napa, (707) 258-1827
- **Grace's Table:** 1400 2nd St., Napa, (707) 226-6200

Adjust according to your tour plans at Robert Mondavi Winery. If you plan to take the 10:00 a.m. winery tour, then you will need to be on the road just after 9:30 a.m. If you plan to take the 11:00 a.m. tour, then you have more time to spare. Leave a bit early, though, so you can enjoy the grounds of the winery when you arrive.

9:30 am -- Drive to Robert Mondavi Winery

- **Price:** FREE
- **Duration:** 30 minutes

We will take Highway 29 North about 12 miles to arrive at Robert Mondavi Winery for a tour and tasting.

10:00 am -- Tour & Tasting at Robert Mondavi Winery

- **Price:** $15.00 (for a single adult)
- **Duration:** 2 hours
- **Address:** 7801 St. Helena Hwy Napa, CA 94574

The experience you have at Robert Mondavi Winery depends on the tour you choose. There are four options:

1) Signature Tour and Tasting, 75 mins, $30, offered at various times

2) Discovery Tour, 30 mins., $15, offered at various times

3) Wine Tasting Basics, 45 mins., $20, begins at 10:00 a.m.

4) Exclusive Cellar, 60 mins., $55, begins at 11:00 a.m. (my recommendation)

You can find out more and reserve a spot in the tour of your choice at http://robertmondavi.com. Click on Visit Us --> Tours & Tastings.

We begin this day at Robert Mondavi Winery because of the winery's visitor-friendly tour options and focus on wine education, the beauty of the property, and commitment to the greater region. For example, Robert Mondavi donated $10 million to build the Mondavi Center for the Arts at the nearby University of California at Davis. The winery has a long history in Napa Valley, and he played a strong role in developing Napa Valley into one of the world's leading wine producing regions.

Our time at Robert Mondavi Winery is two hours, which allows enough time to fully explore the property and take the tour of your choice. However, you may find that you don't need that much time; in that case, you can adjust accordingly by taking a drive on the nearby roads before or after your tour or driving to St. Helena and browsing the downtown before lunch.

12:00 pm -- Drive to lunch at Gott's Roadside

- **Price:** FREE
- **Duration:** 30 minutes

Take Highway 29 north until just before St. Helena. Look for the **Taylor's Refresher** sign in front of the outdoor restaurant. There is ample parking next to the restaurant.

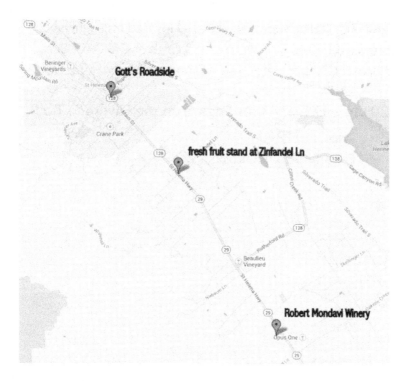

12:30 pm -- Lunch at Gott's Roadside in St. Helena

- **Price:** $35.00 (for a single adult)
- **Duration:** 1 hour and 30 minutes
- **Address:** 933 Main St. Helena, CA 94574

Gott's Roadside is a favorite stop in the area because of its tasty spins on classic American food. The ahi burger, fish tacos, and sweet potato fries are recommended. All seating is outdoors, so if the weather is bad, try one of the following:

If you'd prefer something different, other options include **Solbar** in Calistoga (755 Silverado Trail, $12-20 per plate); **Redd** in Yountville for upscale, seasonal cuisine with ethnic influences (6480 Washington St., Yountville, $12-24 per plate); and **Tra Vigne**, nice Italian food conveniently located on Highway 29 North, just before St. Helena (1050 Charter Oak Ave., St. Helena, $9-32 per plate). See locations on the map for Day 3.

2:00 pm -- Drive to Clos Pegase on the Silverado Trail

- **Price:** FREE
- **Duration:** 15 minutes

Let's make a quick stop at the fruit stand on the side of the road at Hwy 29 and Zinfandel Lane. Much of the year, fresh local fruit can be purchased by leaving money on the honor system.

2:15 pm -- Wine Tasting on the Silverado Trail
- **Price:** $60.00 (for a single adult)
- **Duration:** 2 hours and 45 minutes
- **Address:** 1060 Dunaweal Ln, Calistoga, CA 94515

The **Silverado Trail** and the small roads that connect it with Highway 29 have many lovely wineries. We will begin next to Calistoga at **Clos Pegase Winery**. This winery is known for its unusual architecture and collection of fine art and sculpture, which is free and open to the public.

The winery's owner, Jan Shrem, is devoted to making art available to the public -- he recently donated $10 million to build a new art museum on the campus of nearby UC Davis. Tastings at Clos Pegase range between $20 and $30 depending on the flight of wines, but the highlight here is the winery's combination of fine art and wine.

Let's continue down the Silverado Trail for our next stop.

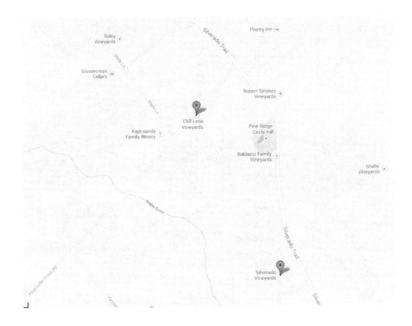

We will continue to a couple of smaller wineries. First, **Cliff Lede Vineyards** is a small winery with comfortable seating, outdoor gardens, and sculptures by well-known 20th-century artist Jim Dine. It is located just off the Silverado Trail at 1473 Yountville Cross Rd.

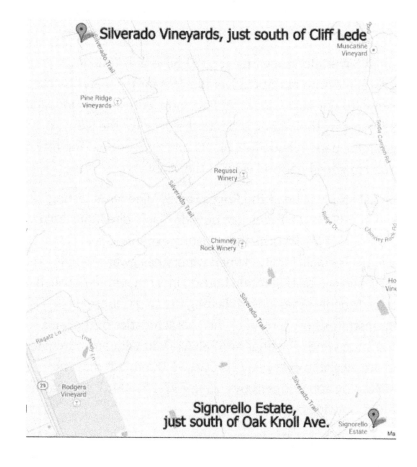

We have probably had enough wine right now, so our next stop will be for the views. Near Cliff Lede are two hilltop wineries with some of the valley's nicest overlooks, especially in the fall when the vineyard leaves change colors. In fact, from Silverado Vineyards, you can see the colors of different types of grape vines -- patches of purple, red, orange, and yellow produce a striking pattern in the vineyards below the hilltop winery.

Stop at **Silverado Vineyards** at 6121 Silverado Trail or **Signorello Estate** at 4500 Silverado Trail for the views before heading to our next winery. At Silverado, enter the winery and continue past the tasting room to the deck for the view. At Signorello, park outside the winery and walk around the row of shrubs to get a beautiful view of the vineyards.

Our last stop will be at the **Rocca Family Vineyards** tasting room at 129 Devlin Road, just outside Napa (directions below). This is one of my favorite wine tasting experiences in Napa Valley! This small, family-owned winery has award-winning red wines, and the tasting room, housed in a renovated house, has a cozy, friendly atmosphere. Tasting the two Cabernets demonstrates how terroir, or the characteristics of the land, affects the wines. Tastings are $35 (waived with any purchase) and are available every day 10:00am-5:00pm but must be reserved by appointment by calling 707-257-8467 or emailing info@roccawines.com.

Directions to Rocca Family Vineyards: From Signorello Estate (or from anywhere on Silverado Trail), turn left to continue south on Silverado Trail. After 3 miles, turn left onto Trancas and then right onto Silverado Trail. After almost 3 miles, turn left onto Soscol Ave/CA 121-S. Soon after, CA 121-S becomes Napa

Vallejo Hwy CA 221-S. Continue south for about 3 more miles. When this intersects with Hwy 12, just continue straight onto Soscol Ave. Take the first left onto Devlin Rd., and Rocca is on right.

5:00 pm -- Drive back to Downtown Napa and Oxbow Public Market

- **Price:** FREE
- **Duration:** 15 minutes

Let's finish our afternoon by driving to Oxbow Public Market in Downtown Napa where we can park in the public parking lot. If you're ready for a nap after this busy day, go back to your accommodation and meet us at Oxbow a little later.

5:15 pm -- Oxbow Public Market

- **Price:** $40.00 (for a single adult)
- **Duration:** 1 hour and 45 minutes
- **Address:** 644 1st St, Napa, CA 94559

Oxbow Public Market is a fantastic indoor food market that showcases the variety of local food available in the Napa area. From organic ice cream and artisan chocolates to Neapolitan pizza and local cheeses, the quality of the food and related products is high. Highly recommended restaurants include **Kitchen Door**, **Hog Island Oyster Bar**, and **C Casa**. For a sweet treat, choose from **Three Twins** ice cream, **Kara's Cupcakes**, and the incredible organic pastries on display at **Ca' Momi** (try the bignés).

Be sure to find out, either on the website or at the market, if there is a Happy Hour event this day. Locals' nights occur every Tuesday from 5:00 - 8:00 p.m., and Happy Hour also happens at select purveyors on other days.

This is also a great place for us to shop for gifts and souvenirs from Napa Valley, especially locally made olive oil at **The Olive Press** and chocolates at **Anette's Chocolates.**

7:00 pm -- Return to accommodation (or hit the town)

- **Price:** FREE
- **Duration:** 2 hours
- **Address:** Downtown Napa

We've had a busy day, so you may be ready to relax at your accommodation. If not, enjoy an evening in Downtown Napa.

It's the end of our 3-day stay in Napa Valley. We've visited some of the best of what Napa Valley has to offer, from downtown tasting rooms and beautiful hillside wineries to food markets and some of the region's best restaurants. After our busy last day, you may be ready for a relaxing evening. If not, here are some ideas for a fun last evening in Napa Valley:

- Stop by **Morimoto Napa** for a cocktail.
- Have a late dinner at any of the fine restaurants you haven't tried yet: **ZuZu, Tarla Mediterranean Grill, Grace's Table,Eiko's** (Japanese), or **Carpe Diem.**
- Use your **Downtown Napa Wine Tasting Card** at any of the remaining tasting rooms that are open in the evenings.
- Check out Napa's live music scene at **Silo's** (530 Main St. next to Napa River Inn), where you can watch live jazz with a glass of wine or cocktail and an appetizer.
- Try **Carpe Diem's wine bar** or the **John Anthony tasting room** for a late night glass of wine.

Things You Need to Know (Appendix)

Before you go

Making Reservations:

Pre-book a winery tour on the Wine Train (optional): http://winetrain.com/winery-tours

Reservations for meals and some activities are recommended: (See the itinerary for each day for specific information about each restaurant and activity.)

For dinner on Day 1: Morimoto Napa 707-252-1600, Grace's Table 707-226-6200, or ZuZu 707-224-8555

For Day 2 spa treatment: Baths at Roman Spa 1-800-914-8957, or Solage Calistoga 707-226-0800

Day 2 optional wine tasting in Calistoga: Bennett Lane Winery 1-877-MAX-NAPA to make a reservation.

Day 2 dinner: Oenotri 707-252-1022. If Oenotri is full or you don't feel like Italian, try Tarla Mediterranean Grill 707-255-5599.

Day 3 winery tour at Robert Mondavi: Reserve a spot in the tour of your choice at http://robertmondavi.com, click on Visit Us --> Tours & Tastings.

Day 3 wine tasting at Rocca Family Vineyards' tasting room: 707-257-8467 or email info@roccawines.com for a reservation.

Accommodation recommendations:

The Napa River Inn: Napa's only Michelin-starred hotel, the Napa River Inn is in the old mill building from the late 19th century and sits on the lovely Napa Riverfront. The hotel is a charming historic registry building and prides itself on great service and it's on site spa.

The Beazley House: Napa's oldest B&B is located within walking distance of Downtown Napa on a pleasant residential street. Request the carriage house rooms -- they are spacious, quiet, and comfortable.

The Inn on First: Also within walking distance of Downtown Napa, this B&B is modern and luxurious and boasts the best B&B breakfast in Napa. Highly recommended also for the owners' helpfulness in choosing where to eat and what to do and their commitment to being green.

Restaurant recommendations:

Napa Valley is one of the country's best areas for food, and there are many high-quality places to eat. While specific recommendations are given in the itinerary, this list includes personal favorites as well as long-time favorites of locals and frequent visitors.

The Kitchen Door, Oxbow Public Market, Napa: Some of Napa's best food comes from this restaurant located in Oxbow Public Market.

Hog Island Oysters, Oxbow Public Market, Napa: Oysters from the coast west of Napa Valley are served at the bar and tables in this casual location inside the Oxbow Public Market, Downtown Napa

Bouchon Bistro, Yountville: Thomas Keller's famous food in a casual, less expensive location.

Carpe Diem, Napa: Diverse menu in a youthful atmosphere in Downtown Napa. Try their special tacos.

Zuzu, Napa: Spanish-style tapas in a lively atmosphere in Downtown Napa

Oenotri, Napa: Italian food in Downtown Napa. One of my favorites.

All Seasons Bistro, Calistoga: Focused on local, seasonal food, this restaurant has been here for more than 30 years with excellent salads, wine pairings, and decadent desserts.

Calistoga Kitchen, Calistoga: A small menu showcasing smoothies and sophisticated food with seasonal ingredients. The duck soup is their specialty.

Solbar (especially for breakfast), Calistoga

Grace's Table, Napa: Fresh food with an international flair served at breakfast, lunch, dinner, and Happy Hour. This is my favorite restaurant in Downtown Napa! Super fresh ingredients including vegetables and herbs from the chef's garden.

Eiko's, Napa: Elegant Japanese food in Downtown Napa

Morimoto, Napa: Upscale Japanese food on the Downtown Napa Riverfront, this is Iron Chef Morimoto's restaurant.

Wine Tasting Tips:

1) *How much?* Wine tasting in Napa Valley is expensive. Tastings are usually $20-40 per person, though many wineries waive the tasting fee with the purchase of a bottle, The Downtown Napa wine tasting card is a great deal at $30 for tastings at 12 locations. It can be purchased online and at the Napa Visitors' Centers.

2) *Where?* Napa Valley has a huge array of wineries, so you should visit ones that suit your interests. Besides the wineries that reflect the best of Napa Valley's wine production, such as the ones listed in this itinerary, you may want to visit others that suit your interests. For example, if you prefer sparkling wines or are interested in architecture, ask for recommendations at the Visitors' Center.

3) *How?* The most common technique includes the following steps:

Step 1: Swirl the wine for a few seconds to let it open. Doing so allows oxygen to enter the wine and release the "nose" of the wine.

Step 2: Stick your nose in the glass and breathe in. Notice the aromas.

Step 3: Take a sip and let it sit in your mouth. Swish the wine around a bit to allow the flavors to be released. Swallow. Repeat and notice how the wine can change as you taste it. If you don't want to swallow the wine, you can spit it into the dump bucket on the counter.

Step 4: When you have had enough of that wine, pour the remainder of the glass into one of the dump buckets located on the tasting counter.

Be sure you have a paper of tasting notes that identify the wines and their profiles. Ask questions about the varietals and where they are grown so you can learn more about California wines.

Some wineries and tasting rooms offer cheese or charcuterie plates for an additional charge. Pairing wine with food adds another dimension to the tasting experience and is highly recommended.

Drink plenty of water during the day. Remember that there are drivers and taxis in case you feel that the wine has gone to your head and you should not drive. Ask the tasting room manager for help arranging a driver.

4) *What?* A wine must be made up of at least 75% of one grape varietal unless it's called a blend. For instance, if you are drinking a 2012 Cabernet Sauvignon, the wine must be at least 75% Cabernet Sauvignon. The remainder may be a blend of other red varietals. So a wine that's labelled Cabernet Sauvignon may be 100% Cabernet Sauvignon or may be a mix of, say, 80% Cabernet Sauvignon, 10% Merlot, 6% Petit Verdot, and 4% Syrah.

Find out more about wine tasting at http://thisismyhappiness.com/2012/06/30/wine-tasting-tips/.

Resources

30 Things to Do in Napa Valley
http://thisismyhappiness.com/2012/07/16/30-things-to-do-in-napa-valley/

Budget Travel Tips for Napa Valley
http://thisismyhappiness.com/2013/09/30/budget-travel-tips-for-napa-valley/

Downtown Napa
http://donapa.com/

Visit Napa Valley
http://www.visitnapavalley.com/welcome_centers.htm

About the Author

Jenna Francisco

I'm a California-based ESL teacher who always wanted to be a travel writer since my early days of traveling Europe and living in the Czech Republic. I've begun to realize my dream through years of researching, blogging and freelance writing, and I'm happy to share my knowledge with others.

My blog, *This Is My Happiness*, focuses on lesser-known places in California and my other favorite destinations, Brazil and Italy. My travels integrate my various interests, from culture and art to wine and landscape. As the parent of two small boys, I'm always looking for ways to travel as a family without sacrificing one ounce of fun, but as a wine lover, I'm always looking for what's new in California wine country.

Twitter: @thismyhappiness

Blog: http://thisismyhappiness.com

Unanchor
Chief Itinerary Coordinator

Unanchor wants your opinion.

Your next travel adventure starts now. A simple review on Amazon will grant you and a travel buddy, friend, or human of your choosing any of the wonderful Unanchor digital itineraries for free.

What a deal!

Leave a review:

* http://www.amazon.com/unanchor

Collect your guides

* Send an email to reviews@unanchor.com with a link to your review.
* Wait with bated breath.
* Receive your new travel adventure in your inbox!

Other Unanchor Itineraries
Africa

- One Day in Africa - A Guide to Tangier
- Johannesburg/Pretoria: A 4-Day South Africa Tour Itinerary
- Cape Town - What not to miss on a 4-day first-timers' itinerary

Asia

- Beijing Must Sees, Must Dos, Must Eats - 3-Day Tour Itinerary
- 2 Days in Shanghai: A Budget-Conscious Peek at Modern China
- Shanghai 3-Day Tour Itinerary
- Between the Skyscrapers - Hong Kong 3-Day Discovery Tour
- 3-Day Budget Delhi Itinerary
- Delhi in 3 Days - A Journey Through Time
- 3 Days Highlights of Mumbai
- A 3-Day Tryst with 300-Year-Old Kolkata
- Kolkata (Calcutta): 2 Days of Highlights
- Art and Culture in Ubud, Bali – 1-Day Highlights
- Go with the Sun to Borobudur & Prambanan in 1 Day
- Nozawa Onsen's Winter Secrets - A 3-Day Tour
- Tour Narita During an Airport Layover
- 3-Day Highlights of Tokyo
- 3 Days in the Vibrant City of Seoul and the Serene Countryside of Gapyeong

- Manila on a Budget: 2-Day Itinerary
- A 3-Day Thrilla in Manila then Flee to the Sea
- The Very Best of Moscow in 3 Days
- Saint Petersburg in Three Days
- Family Friendly Singapore - 3 Days in the Lion City
- The Affordable Side of Singapore: A 4-Day Itinerary
- A First Timer's Guide to 3 Days in the City that Barely Sleeps - Singapore
- Singapore: 3 Fun-Filled Days on this Tiny Island
- The Two Worlds of Kaohsiung in 5 Days
- 72 Hours in Taipei: The All-rounder
- The Ins and Outs of Bangkok: A 3-Day Guide
- Girls' Weekend in Bangkok: Shop, Spa, Savour, Swoon
- Saigon 3-Day Beyond the Guidebook Itinerary

Central America

- Your Chiapas Adventure: San Cristobal de las Casas and Palenque, Mexico 5-Day Itinerary
- Mexico City 3-Day Highlights Itinerary
- Everything to see or do in Mexico City - 7-Day Itinerary
- Todo lo que hay que ver o hacer en la Ciudad de México - Itinerario de 7 Días
- Cancun and Mayan Riviera 5-Day Itinerary (3rd Edition)

Europe
France

- Paris to Chartres Cathedral: 1-Day Tour Itinerary
- A 3-Day Tour of Mont St Michel, Normandy and Brittany
- Paris 4-Day Winter Wonderland
- The Best of Paris in One Day
- Paris 1-Day Itinerary - Streets of Montmartre
- Paris 3-Day Walking Tour: See Paris Like a Local
- Paris for Free: 3 Days
- Art Lovers' Paris: A 2-Day Artistic Tour of the City of Lights

Italy

- Discover Rome's Layers: A 3-Day Walking Tour
- A 3-Day Tour Around Ancient Rome
- 3 Days of Roman Adventure: spending time and money efficiently in Rome
- A Day on Lake Como, Italy
- Milan Unknown - A 3-day tour itinerary
- Landscape, Food, & Trulli: 1 Week in Puglia, the Valle d'Itria, and Matera
- 3-Day Florence Walking Tours
- Florence, Italy 3-Day Art & Culture Itinerary
- See Siena in a Day
- Three Romantic Walks in Venice

Spain

- Málaga, Spain – 2-Day Tour from the Moors to Picasso
- Mijas - One Day Tour of an Andalucían White Village
- Two-Day Tour in Sunny Seville, Spain
- FC Barcelona: More than a Club (A 1-Day Experience)
- 3-Day Highlights of Barcelona Itinerary
- Ibiza on a Budget - Three-Day Itinerary
- Three days exploring Logroño and La Rioja by public transport
- Best of Valencia 2-Day Guide

United Kingdom
England
London

- 3-Day London Tour for Olympic Visitors
- London's Historic City Wall Walk (1-2 days)
- London 1-Day Literary Highlights
- The 007 James Bond Day Tour of London
- An Insider's Guide to the Best of London in 3 Days
- Done London? A 3-day itinerary for off the beaten track North Norfolk
- London's South Bank - Off the Beaten Track 1-Day Tour
- London for Free :: Three-Day Tour
- London's Villages - A 3-day itinerary exploring Hampstead, Marylebone and Notting Hill
- Low-Cost, Luxury London - 3-Day Itinerary
- Bath: An Exploring Guide - 2-Day Itinerary
- 2-Day Brighton Best-of Walks & Activities
- Bristol in 2 Days: A Local's Guide
- MADchester - A Local's 3-Day Guide To Manchester
- One Day in Margate, UK on a Budget

Rest of the UK

- History, Culture, and Craic: 3 Days in Belfast, Ireland
- The Best of Edinburgh: A 3-Day Journey from Tourist to Local
- Two-Day Self-Guided Walks - Cardiff

Rest of Europe

- 3 Days in Brussels - The grand sites via the path less trodden
- Zagreb For Art Lovers: A Three-Day Itinerary
- 3-Day Prague Beer Pilgrimage
- Best of Prague - 3-Day Itinerary
- 3 Days in Helsinki
- Weekend Break: Tbilisi - Crown Jewel of the Caucasus
- 2 Days In Berlin On A Budget
- A 3-Day Guide to Berlin, Germany
- Athens 3-Day Highlights Tour Itinerary
- Chania & Sfakia, Greece & Great Day Trips Nearby (5-Day Itinerary)
- Day Trip From Thessaloniki to Kassandra Peninsula, Halkidiki, Greece
- 2-Day Beach Tour: Travel like a Local in Sithonia Peninsula, Halkidiki, Greece
- Thessaloniki, Greece - 3-Day Highlights Itinerary
- 3 Days in Dublin City - City Highlights, While Eating & Drinking Like a Local
- Amsterdam 3-Day Alternative Tour: Not just the Red Light District
- Amsterdam Made Easy: A 3-Day Guide
- Two-day tour of Utrecht: the smaller, less touristy Amsterdam!

- Krakow: Three-Day Tour of Poland's Cultural Capital
- Best of Warsaw 2-Day Itinerary
- Lisbon in 3 Days: Budget Itinerary
- Braşov - Feel the Pulse of Transylvania in 3 Days
- Lausanne 1-Day Tour Itinerary

Middle East

- Adventure Around Amman: A 2-Day Itinerary
- Amman 2-Day Cultural Tour
- 3 Days as an Istanbulite: An Istanbul Itinerary
- Between the East and the West, a 3-Day Istanbul Itinerary

North America
United States
California

- Orange County 3-Day Budget Itinerary
- Beverly Hills, Los Angeles - 1-Day Tour
- Los Angeles On A Budget - 4-Day Tour Itinerary
- Los Angeles 4-Day Itinerary (partly using Red Tour Bus)
- Downtown Los Angeles 1-Day Walking Tour
- Sunset Strip, Los Angeles - 1-Day Walking Tour
- 2-Day Los Angeles Vegan and Vegetarian Foodie Itinerary
- Los Angeles Highlights 3-Day Itinerary
- Hollywood, Los Angeles - 1-Day Walking Tour
- Wine, Food, and Fun: 3 Days in Napa Valley
- Beyond the Vine: 2-Day Napa Tour
- Palm Springs, Joshua Tree & Salton Sea: A 3-Day Itinerary

- RVA Haunts, History, and Hospitality: Three Days in Richmond, Virginia
- Best of the Best: Three-Day San Diego Itinerary
- San Francisco Foodie Weekend Itinerary
- San Francisco 2-Day Highlights Itinerary
- The Tech Lover's 48-Hour Travel Guide to Silicon Valley & San Francisco
- Three Days in Central California's Wine Country

New York

- Brooklyn, NY 2-Day Foodie Tour
- A Local's Guide to Montauk, New York in 2 Days - From the Ocean to the Hills
- Day Trip from New York City: Mountains, Falls, & a Funky Town
- Jewish New York in Two Days
- Lower Key, Lower Cost: Lower Manhattan - 1-Day Itinerary
- Hidden Bars of New York City's East Village & Lower East Side: A 2-Evening Itinerary
- New York Like A Native: Five Boroughs in Six Days
- New York City - First Timer's 2-Day Walking Tour
- 3-Day Amazing Asian Food Tour of New York City!
- New York City's Lower East Side, 1-Day Tour Itinerary
- Weekend Tour of Portland's Craft Breweries, Wineries, & Distilleries
- Day Trip from New York City: Heights of the Hudson Valley (Bridges and Ridges)

Rest of the USA

- Alaska Starts Here - 3 Days in Seward
- The Best of Phoenix & Scottsdale: 3-Day Itinerary

- Tucson: 3 Days at the Intersection of Mexico, Native America & the Old West
- The Best of Boulder, CO: A Three-Day Guide
- Louisville: Three Days in Derby City
- A Local's Guide to the Hamptons 3 Day Itinerary
- New Haven Highlights: Art, Culture & History 3-Day Itinerary
- 2 Days Exploring Haunted Key West
- 3-Day Discover Orlando Itinerary
- Three Days in the Sunshine City of St. Petersburg, Florida
- Atlanta 3-Day Highlights
- Savannah 3-Day Highlights Itinerary
- Lesser-known Oahu in 4 Days on a Budget
- Local's Guide to Oahu - 3-Day Tour Itinerary
- Tackling 10 Must-Dos on the Big Island in 3 Days
- Chicago Food, Art and Funky Neighborhoods in 3 Days
- 3-Day Chicago Highlights Itinerary
- 6-Hour "Layover" Chicago
- Famous Art & Outstanding Restaurants in Chicago 1-Day Itinerary
- Beer Lovers 3-Day Guide To Northern California
- The Best of Kansas City: 3-Day Itinerary
- Day Trek Along the Hudson River
- Wichita From Cowtown to Air Capital in 2 Days
- La Grange, Kentucky: A 3-Day Tour Itinerary
- Paris Foodie Classics: 1 Day of French Food
- New Orleans 3-Day Itinerary
- Weekend Day Trip from New York City: The Wine & Whiskey Trail
- Baltimore: A Harbor, Parks, History, Seafood & Art - 3-Day Itinerary

- Navigating Centuries of Boston's Nautical History in One Day
- Rainy Day Boston One-Day Itinerary
- Boston 2-Day Historic Highlights Itinerary
- Summer in Jackson Hole: Local Tips for the Perfect Three to Five Day Adventure
- Las Vegas - Gaming Destination Diversions - Ultimate 3-Day Itinerary
- Las Vegas on a Budget - 3-Day Itinerary
- Cruisin' Asbury like a Local in 1 Day
- Girls' 3-Day Weekend Summer Getaway in Asheville, NC
- Five Days in the Wild Outer Banks of North Carolina
- Family Weekend in Columbus, OH
- Ohio State Game Day Weekend
- Portland Bike and Bite: A 2-Day Itinerary
- Three Days Livin' as a True and Local Portlander
- A Laid-Back Long Weekend in Austin, TX
- 3 Day PA Dutch Country Highlights (Lancaster County, PA)
- Two Days in Philadelphia
- Pittsburgh: Three Days Off the Beaten Path
- Corpus Christi: The Insider Guide for a 4-Day Tour
- An Active 2-3 Days In Moab, Utah
- The Weekenders Guide To Burlington, Vermont
- Washington, DC in 4 Days
- Washington, DC: 3 Days Like a Local
- A Day on Bainbridge Island

Canada

- Relax in Halifax for Two Days Like a Local
- The Best of Toronto - 2-Day Itinerary

- An Insider's Guide to Toronto: Explore the City Less Traveled in Three Days
- Toronto: A Multicultural Retreat (3-day itinerary)

Oceania
Australia

- Two Wheels and Pair of Cozzies: the Best of Newcastle in 3 Days
- A Weekend Snapshot of Sydney
- Sydney, Australia - 3-Day **Best Of** Itinerary
- The Blue Mountains: A weekend of nature, culture and history.
- Laneway Melbourne: A One-Day Walking Tour
- Magic of Melbourne 3-Day Tour
- A Weekend Snapshot of Melbourne
- An Afternoon & Evening in Melbourne's Best Hidden Bars
- Best of Perth's Most Beautiful Sights in 3 Days

New Zealand

- Enjoy the Rebuild - Christchurch 2-Day Tour
- The Best of Wellington: 3-Day Itinerary

South America

- An Insider's Guide to the Best of Buenos Aires in 3 Days
- Buenos Aires Best Kept Secrets: 2-Day Itinerary
- Sights & Sounds of São Paulo - 3-Day Itinerary
- A 1-Day Foodie's Dream Tour of Arequipa
- Arequipa - A 2-Day Itinerary for First-Time Visitors
- Cusco and the Sacred Valley - a five-day itinerary for a first-time visitor

- Little Known Lima 3-Day Tour

Unanchor is a global family for travellers to experience the world with the heart of a local.

Made in the
USA
Monee, IL